NAVIGATING THE TRANSITION

A Guide to Moving from Education to Occupation

CHARLES L. JONES

PRESS

Navigating the Transition: A Guide to Moving from Education to Occupation

Copyright © 2023 Charles L. Jones

Published by StoryBuilders Press

Paperback: 978-1-954521-19-3
Ebook: 978-1-954521-20-9

I dedicate this book to my daughters, Tiffany and Eryka, and to all young people just stepping out into their careers. You have an exciting journey ahead of you, and I am honored to be a small part of it!

TABLE OF CONTENTS

CHAPTER 1

THE PRE-EXPLORATION STAGE OF THE CAREER LIFE CYCLE

In my journey as a Human Resources Executive, talent acquisition and campus recruiting were top priorities in the hiring process. More often than not, when an HR representative from a prominent company is on campus during college recruiting events, their goal is to actively seek out students with high GPAs (3.0 or better) and those who are prepared for the next stage in their lives.

During recruiting events, students I encounter tend to ask questions such as, "What is a good GPA?", "How do I prepare for the real world?", "What should I expect after graduation?", and "What classes should I take to be ready for my career?"

My answer in most cases is, "Well, that depends." I tell students there are no silver bullets. My own career path was set before I even graduated because I enrolled in the Reserve Officer Training Corps (ROTC) and was commissioned as a 2nd Lieutenant in the US Army. I did not experience the normal stresses of having to find a job or wonder about a career.

In most cases, though, you will have to chart your own course. But if you are dedicated and determined, you will definitely make progress. I also tell them that time is their most valuable asset, and I caution them to use it wisely.

When I say use time wisely, here's what I mean: When it's time to study, time to focus, you need to be very intentional about giving everything the very best of you. Whether it's a project, a test, or anything to do with your education, take the time to give it your all. Never allow yourself to go halfway, and never do just enough, always go above and beyond. Trust me, it will pay off.

Another good use of your time is joining clubs or groups. Not only does it get you involved, but it also builds your resume. (More on this later).

Things to avoid include staying away from or limiting the amount of time you spend around individuals that don't have your shared goal. There will be some friends you make that are in college for fun, not focus. While it can be very tempting to play around, know when the right time is for it, and when it's time to buckle down and get serious.

I recall returning to my alma mater, Jackson State University, an HBCU (Historically Black College or University), to recruit graduating seniors from the College of Business. I interviewed several students with GPAs of 3.0 or higher. They met my company's recruiting requirements and were well-prepared for their next stage.

However, I also interviewed several students with GPAs between 2.5-2.9, who were not as well-prepared. As a representative of my company, I told these students that a 3.0 GPA is important, and, in most cases, it's the cost of entry. However, I also explained that I was more seeking "Holistic Students." These individuals do not necessarily need a 3.0 GPA to be recruited and hired. But, if they do not have it, there should be plenty of evidence of strengths and talents in other areas.

I needed to hear from these candidates what they were doing to prepare for their careers, as well as the reasons their GPAs were less than 3.0. Some questions that I asked included:

- ➤ Do you have a career plan?
- ➤ Is your major or degree your passion?
- ➤ Have you researched your field of study or industry?
- ➤ Have you done research on the company before interviewing?
- ➤ Do you have an alumni mentor?
- ➤ Have you completed an internship, either paid or not paid?
- ➤ Are you actively participating in on-campus organizations?
- ➤ What leadership roles did you have?
- ➤ How well do you adapt to different cultures or environments?
- ➤ Are you working a part-time job?
- ➤ How successful are you at networking?
- ➤ Can you assimilate or adapt to challenges?
- ➤ How do you overcome obstacles?

The statistics on students feeling unprepared for the "real world" (nearly 74%) and entering college as undecided freshmen (more than 50%) are alarming.[1] It is not uncommon for students to feel overwhelmed and unsure about their future career paths.[2] However, it is important to recognize that these feelings are not unique to college students. Many individuals struggle with career decisions and feeling prepared for the workforce, regardless of their level of education or experience.

There are a number of reasons why students may feel so unprepared. For some, it may be a lack of exposure to different career options or a lack of guidance on how to explore their interests and passions. Others may struggle with time management or independent learning, which can make the transition to college or the workforce challenging.

It is also important to recognize that not all students will have the same level of preparation or support when entering college or the workforce. Some students may come from disadvantaged backgrounds or face other challenges that impact their ability to succeed. Providing resources and support for these students can help to level the playing field and ensure that all students have access to the opportunities they need to succeed.

Pre-Exploration Stage of the Career Life Cycle

What's missing for many young people entering college or trade school, or going straight from high school into a job, is what I call the Pre-Exploration Stage of the Career Life

Cycle. This is a time when you should do a deep dive into an understanding of what your passions and purpose are for your life, pinpointing a career that has the potential to be fulfilling, but also to provide you with the lifestyle you hope to achieve.

For some, college can be a great opportunity to explore your interests and passions, and to determine what you want for your future. My daughter, Tiffany, for example, knew she wanted to do something involved with science, possibly medicine, but didn't feel completely ready to take the leap into medical school. She was fearful she wasn't prepared—and, if we are being honest, she wasn't.

The transition from high school to college can be a challenging experience for many students. They don't fully understand how to study independently in order to teach themselves all of the content covered in their courses. It is definitely a learning curve. It can be a huge shock and wake-up call.

Explore your options. The old traditions of graduating high school and attending a four-year university are not only dated, but are unnecessary for some individuals and career paths. The options for a less expensive—yet equally valuable—education are far too often overlooked.

Take for example a family friend, Alex. During his junior and senior years of high school, he was able to choose his elective classes, which led him to welding and machining. He found that he really enjoyed working with his hands, creating things from raw materials, and manipulating them until they were a finished product.

After junior year he knew it was definitely something he was interested in pursuing. He talked with his teacher to see what opportunities were available for him to start getting his foot in the door. His teacher pointed in the direction of a local manufacturing company that was heavily involved with student development and did job fairs in the area. Alex was able to meet with one of the owners and arrange to work part-time during his open class periods. It gave him part-time work while he was in school and afforded some hands-on experience in his area of interest.

When he realized how much he enjoyed the work he was doing, Alex spoke with his teacher again about schooling options. There were options to follow at a traditional four-year college in manufacturing, but his teacher encouraged him to consider a trade school program at an area community college. Alex knew after touring the campus and learning about the curriculum that it was a perfect fit, so he applied. While he worked at applying for scholarships, unbeknownst to him, his teacher had submitted him as a candidate for the Molex scholarship, which would cover the majority of his expenses. He was more than elated to be selected and have all of his tuition paid. All he had left to cover were books and room and board.

The program taught Alex everything he needed to become proficient in machining, while also providing his necessary general education courses, and assisting in his job search. Although the market in his area was slim for machinists, he was able to land a job just a few months after graduation which led him to a successful career as a machinist and test technician. All of this happened in just two years.

Where You Start Isn't Necessarily Where You Should Finish

I have another young friend, AJ Wilson. His story isn't one that started off very bright, but has since led him to a fulfilling and successful career. AJ started off college at the University of Missouri, but quickly found that he wasn't prepared for the experience. For his second semester, he switched to a local community college. He felt it was a better fit for him as it helped him transition from the learning styles of high school to college.

I remember him telling me that he believes everyone can find value in attending a community college for at least a year. He told me he believes this because there are valuable lessons to be learned unless you are going into college with a good head on your shoulders and are truly grounded in your self-motivation to study and learn on your own. The appeal of community college is that while it doesn't have the "sparkle and shine" of a university, they offer professors and programs at the same level with a lower price tag and a more intimate setting.

AJ moved on from community college to Illinois State. During that time he took part in an internship in a warehouse which led to his current career as a materials manager with an aerospace company. That internship gave him real-life experience, and a shoo-in for the industry, to bring him to his career.

If nothing else, the journey toward exploration of further education and career is an experience in self-development. It is in this experience you will begin to understand what motivation looks like. Sometimes this comes in the form of failure. But it is within that failure that you will find an appreciation for discipline, consistency, reliability, follow-through, and integrity—all the life skills you needed, not only to perform in your career, but to live your life.

The Power of Possibility Questions:

- ✓ If you're still in school, what is your current GPA?
- ✓ If it is below 3.0, how much time do you have left to bump it up before graduating?
- ✓ What positive things do you do outside of class that may take away from your study time but also help prepare you for your future?
- ✓ Are you interested in a corporate career, skilled technical work, entrepreneurship, or something else after school? What interests you about that?

CHAPTER 2

DETERMINING LIFE PURPOSE

I remember my daughter, Tiffany, struggling to find her passion and purpose early on. She felt a tremendous amount of pressure from outside or external influences, such as the expectations of her family, her friends, and her peers. If you ask her today about her experience, she will openly share that she now recognizes she was nowhere near mature enough at the ages of 18 to 22 to be able to truly discern what she wanted for her life or what she was meant to do.

Tiffany felt pulled in two different directions—science and teaching. She loved everything about science, especially conducting experiments. She also loved sharing her knowledge with others and felt teaching would be a great fit. At first, she majored in genetics with the intention to become a science teacher. Over time, and with some other experiences, she realized she was meant to pursue medicine. It has since become the perfect fit for her purpose, as she works in a laboratory setting conducting experiments and teaching fellow medical students at Johns Hopkins.

Many young people begin their career journey with financial success as their measuring stick. Unfortunately, with time, they find that wealth doesn't necessarily bring them happiness or a sense of purpose or meaning. This is why I can't stress enough to those that seek my advice to begin your journey with purpose and passion as your benchmark. But how can you know your purpose, especially as someone just finishing school?

This difference between a job and a career is all about mindset. If you are there to take up space and earn a paycheck, it's just a job. A career is something that brings you a sense of deep joy and fulfillment; it fits your life purpose.

A job with material gains as the only focus lacks significance. It lacks the purpose of working for the greater good or in the service of others and makes cultivating meaningful working relationships difficult or impossible. While your bank account may be full, your success isn't really success at all. It is superficial and disingenuous.

My best advice for you as you navigate the Pre-Exploration Stage of your Career Life Cycle is to find something you're passionate about and explore the opportunities to turn it into a career. No matter what it is, if you go all in, you will increase your likelihood of success.

A great way to explore during this stage is through service and giving back. This could very well be where you find your passion and purpose in life. Through the act of serving others, you can build empathy and emotional intelligence.[1]

Once my daughter, Tiffany, decided on medicine as her field of study, she minored in global health. Part of that program was visiting other countries to learn how others practice medicine and more about their healthy eating habits. She visited Uganda for a month and a half where her group stopped in a variety of villages. They observed them preparing food and assisted in serving the tribes. It afforded her the opportunity to learn more about other cultures and interact with others.

Throughout this opportunity, Tiffany discovered the importance of making connections with others in order to develop trust. While many students went on those visits to check a box to obtain their degrees, Tiffany found a deeper, more meaningful connection that helped her to grow, not only as a medical provider, but also as a person. She developed a greater understanding of her purpose here on Earth—what she was made to do in the world and who she is serving. It gave her an overall feeling of joy in her day-to-day work, creating a deep purpose in her work that goes beyond the paycheck.

A practical approach to finding your career path is to seek the assistance of the career offices at your trade school, college, or university. Often they have staff that is trained in helping you narrow your skills, passions, and abilities to find potentially successful career options. Many times they offer placement assessments as a tool that dives a bit deeper into your natural abilities, maybe even some you wouldn't naturally gravitate towards.

A few assessments you could consider might include:

➤ Myers-Briggs Type Indicator (MBTI): The MBTI is a personality assessment that can help individuals to identify their personality type and preferred work style. This can be a useful tool for identifying potential career paths that align with one's personality and preferences.

➤ Strong Interest Inventory (SII): The SII is a career assessment that measures an individual's interests in different occupational areas. This can help individuals to identify potential career paths that align with their interests.

➤ Holland Code Career Test: The Holland Code Career Test is a career assessment that helps individuals to identify their personality type and preferred work environment. This can be a useful tool for identifying potential career paths that align with one's personality and preferences.

➤ CliftonStrengths: CliftonStrengths is a strength assessment that helps individuals to identify their top strengths and talents. This can be a useful tool for identifying potential career paths that align with one's strengths and talents.

➤ Career Key: Career Key is a career assessment that helps individuals to identify their personality type and preferred work environment, and provides information on potential career paths and industries that align with one's interests and values.

It's important to note that career assessments are not a one-size-fits-all solution, and should be used in conjunction with other strategies for identifying potential career paths. It's also important to work with a career counselor or mentor who can help interpret the results of the assessment and provide guidance on potential career paths.

The Power of Possibility Questions:

✓ Everyone defines success differently. What does it mean to you?

✓ In what ways have you participated in service to others?

✓ If you were independently wealthy, yet still chose to go to work, what would you do?

CHAPTER 3

RESEARCHING FOR THE FUTURE

Watching my two daughters decide on their future careers couldn't have been a more diverse experience. Eryka knew exactly what she was going to do at the ripe age of twelve, while Tiffany took her time deciding while she attended college.

My wife and I enrolled Eryka in an organization called Jack and Jill of America, Inc. which held events for African American kids who attended predominantly White middle and high schools. At one of their leadership events, a guest speaker attorney from Universal Studios captured my daughter's attention. The attorney told the students how at the moment her job was to ensure that Universal Studios didn't have any copyright infringements with Disney for the movie *Snow White and the Huntsman*. Eryka was captivated, not only by the amazing suit the attorney wore but by her description of her job. Eryka knew right then and there that she wanted to go to law school and focus on intellectual property, just like the guest speaker.

The problem was, she wasn't sure how she was going to get there. Many pre-law students study criminology because it is the most direct connection. Eryka didn't want to go that path. Instead, she researched how she could turn her love for writing into an undergraduate degree. Thanks to Google, she searched for what she could do with an English degree. The options she found were working for a publishing company or pursuing a law degree. It was a perfect, and natural, fit for her.

After digging even deeper into the potential degrees she could pursue, she decided she would declare a double major in English Literature and Creative Writing. Although she wouldn't find many of her fellow pre-law students with her in these studies, she was beyond ecstatic to be pursuing a degree that fulfilled her passion and her career purpose.

Every year, the students at Eryka's school were encouraged to speak with their study advisors to help keep them on the right track for graduation. At the end of her sophomore year, she went into her meeting thinking she was simply going to be choosing her classes for the next semester. During their discussion, her advisor revealed that she could study abroad and still graduate on time.

There weren't a lot of African American students participating in the study abroad program, so Eryka wasn't sure if it would be a good fit for her. After talking with my wife and me, she decided she would go to Birmingham, England for the second semester of her junior year. She chose England because it paired well with her English literature major. Other students chose Spain or Italy just for fun.

When Eryka arrived in England, she found a huge change in her scenery. Not only was she one of the only African

American students, but she was also one of the few Americans. Due to the political situation and climate at the time, she sometimes lied and said she was from Canada simply to avoid awkwardness!

During her experience, Eryka changed the perspectives of those around her, specifically whatever preconceived notions they had about African American women. She joined a club for barristers, which is what they call lawyers in England. She was afforded the opportunity to travel to seven different countries and made lifelong friendships with her flatmates. It was truly an experience of a lifetime for her.

When she returned from England, she had the mindset that she could pursue law on an international scale. Instead of focusing solely on being a domestic entertainment lawyer, Eryka could venture out and become a contract lawyer for the Cannes Film Festival or work for the BBC. She was given a lens to see the limitless possibilities in front of her.

Tiffany, on the other hand, took her time deciding to become a doctor. She began her collegiate career pursuing an undergraduate degree with a full scholarship. She was pretty sure she wanted to become a science teacher, as she loved sharing her knowledge with others. She always enjoyed the interactions that teaching afforded, plus she loved doing experiments in the science lab.

She decided to major in genetics, which gave her the opportunity to dig deeper into the field of biology. It provided her with the unique experience of a smaller group of fellow students and great mentorships from a brilliant group of professors and advisors.

But eventually, Tiffany changed course and decided that medicine was the direction she wanted to pursue. Since graduating, her work at Johns Hopkins has allowed her to teach others through the residency program, but also do work in the cancer research lab, fulfilling both of her passions.

A family friend's daughter, Shelby, found the beauty of discovering niche work that utilized her career path of law and her love for graphic design. Throughout high school and college, she loved dance and art—both very creative talents. As a law student, she felt limited to pursuing her career in a more corporate setting and putting her creative pursuits aside.

After some detailed research, Shelby found there was a place for her to practice both—intellectual property. Here she is able to fuse art with law. She immediately recognized how much her future changed with this discovery—a rewarding career and happy lifestyle for her future. Shelby recognized that a career in law can lead to a very busy and stressful life, so finding a way to fuse it with her passion will add a level of fun to make it easier to wake up for work each and every day.

Exploring Your Options

When it comes to your future, there is no better way to understand all of your options than research. The best place to start is by reflecting on your long-term goals as best you can—where you want to be, what you aspire to do, and your financial situation. From there you can dive deeper into your options. If you are unsure where to start, a guidance counselor or career coach can help guide you toward helpful resources and give you a path to follow.

The first step, as we discussed earlier, is reflecting on what type of career might best fulfill your passion and purpose, as that will help inform the type of higher education you will want to pursue.

The next step is determining your financial situation before making a decision about your education. If you require financial assistance, researching what is available to you is important. From grants to scholarships and student loans, there is a lot to consider.

Grants are typically awarded based on financial need and do not need to be repaid. They are often provided by federal and state governments, as well as colleges and universities. You can apply for grants by filling out the Free Application for Federal Student Aid (FAFSA) form at FAFSA.gov.

Scholarships are another type of financial aid that students do not need to repay. Scholarships are usually awarded based on academic achievement, athletic ability, or other talents. Scholarships can be provided by a variety of organizations, including colleges, private foundations, and corporations.

Loans, on the other hand, are funds that students borrow to pay for their education and are expected to pay back, usually with interest. Loans can be provided by the federal government or private lenders. It's important for you to carefully consider the terms of all loans before accepting them, as you will need to repay the amount borrowed plus interest over time.

When you have an idea of what type of education you can afford, and have options for financially supporting yourself, begin researching the different types of colleges, trade schools, and universities. You may find that one is the best fit, or a combination of them is your best option.

Only one-third of undergraduate students in 2022 were enrolled in community colleges, despite the potential for huge financial savings.[1]

While only ten percent of community colleges offer a four-year baccalaureate degree, they do offer two-year associate degrees with the opportunity to transfer credits toward a four-year degree.[2] Some of the benefits of community college include:

➤ Lower fees
➤ Flexible schedules
➤ Transferrable credits
➤ Job-focused training
➤ Trade school for specific jobs

The cost implications for community college versus traditional universities are as follows:

	In-State Tuition	Out-of-State Tuition
Community College	$5155	$8835
Private Community College[3]	$15477	–
University	$21370	$37430
Private University[4]	$48510	–

Remember, your path isn't set just because you begin your education in a particular program or at a particular school. As you take courses and learn more about yourself—your strengths and opportunities—other doors may open for different opportunities. Always keep your mind open to pivoting!

Your best fit may be in a program that doesn't exist within a university setting. Depending on your interests, trade school may be your best option. Not only will it save you money, but it will also give you the hands-on knowledge and experience necessary for the job you want.

Trade schools are educational institutions that provide practical and hands-on training for specific career paths such as welding, plumbing, automotive repair, and many others. Unlike traditional colleges and universities, trade schools offer more focused training and job-specific skills to prepare students for a particular trade or vocation.

They are a great option if you want to enter the workforce quickly and prefer a more hands-on approach to learning. Like community colleges, trade schools often have lower tuition costs and shorter program lengths than traditional four-year universities, making them an affordable and efficient alternative for many students. Trade schools can also lead to lucrative careers, and graduates can often find jobs quickly due to the high demand for skilled workers in many industries.

Whether it's the trade school that best suits your interests, the top undergraduate and graduate education programs for your field of study, or the companies that fit your values and purpose best, you have to do your homework.

Finding the Right Fit

After you have settled on the type of higher education you want to pursue, how can you find the trade school, community college, or university that will best suit your personal needs?

It can feel like a daunting task, but there are several factors to consider that can help make the decision easier. First and foremost, consider your personal interests and goals. Look for schools that offer programs in your chosen field or have a strong reputation in that area. Additionally, consider factors such as location, campus culture, class sizes, and available resources such as financial aid, career services, and student organizations.

Visit the schools in person, attend an open house or tour, and talk to current students and faculty. This will give you a sense of the campus culture, student life, and academic environment. You can also look at online reviews and rankings to get an idea of the school's reputation and track record.

And remember, starting at one school doesn't mean you have to finish there. According to a report by the National Student Clearinghouse Research Center, about 37% of college students transfer at least once before earning their degree.[5]

The Power of Possibility Questions:

✓ What are your long-term goals, and how does your choice of higher education fit into them?

✓ What is your financial situation, and what types of financial aid are available to you?

✓ What are the specific programs and schools that offer education in your chosen field or area of interest, and what factors should you consider when choosing a school, such as location, campus culture, class sizes, and available resources?

CHAPTER 4

EMPHASIS ON ACADEMICS AND EXPERIENCE

Throughout high school, there is an emphasis on grades and your overall GPA in order to be considered for acceptance into a college or trade school if that's the path you choose. The same is often true for graduates of colleges or technical schools who are hoping to land a well-paying job.

While employers consider many other factors in the hiring process, your performance in school still plays a role in your credentials. Your scores in school can also serve as a measurement of your work ethic. This is especially true in competitive job markets, such as finance, health, law, education, and tech fields.

The most important thing to keep in mind as you navigate your education, no matter what type of school you attend, is that performance matters. While the measuring stick of GPA may or may not be as relevant, solid grades, evidence of strong participation, and a strong grasp on concepts learned will make you stand out from the crowd.

Take, for example, two students in the same program. One, James, is very dedicated to his schoolwork, and the other, Isaac, is there to "enjoy the experience," as some students say.

James spends his time outside of classes studying hard and reaching out to his professors for help with any work he finds challenging. He also seeks out opportunities to job shadow professionals in his field of interest and works collaboratively with his fellow students on research projects.

Isaac, on the other hand, barely makes it to class and spends his free time socializing with friends. He works just hard enough to keep the equivalent of a C in his classes. His motto: "Cs get degrees!"

When these two young men begin applying for jobs, James will have a resume filled with professional growth experiences and letters of recommendation from his professors. Isaac will have a basic resume. A potential employer will take notice of James' dedication to his academics and recognize the skills necessary as those of a high-performing employee. He'll be the one to get called for an interview every time.

Grades in the real world may get you in the door, but the experiences gained from being well-rounded speak volumes to potential employers. Having a collection of past employers who can speak highly of you and your work ethic can be your springboard for getting the job of your dreams or continuing further education in graduate school, or beyond.

Eryka in particular found that every job and experience she had before and during college has added value and bolstered her resume. In high school, she worked at a local grocery store making smoothies. In college, she worked for a technology company helping them to write user manuals for their products. Both were great for her because the job of making smoothies put her out of her comfort zone as an introvert, as she was forced to talk to people and develop social skills. The technology writing position helped her to recognize her love for writing, which fed well into her legal career. While both are a bit disjointed in nature, they both planted seeds of inspiration for her future.

As of the writing of this book, Eryka continues to bolster her resume. In limbo between taking her Bar Exam and finding a job in entertainment law, she is working as a clerk for a judge. While it isn't the most interesting or exciting job out there, it provides her with an invaluable level of experience in the law field she wouldn't otherwise have. While clerking, Eryka continues to hone her writing skills, developing as a technical writer. And despite her previously held belief that her smoothie girl job hadn't given her many skills for the future, she found that the customer service skills she acquired translated well in effectively communicating with indigent litigants, attorneys, judges, secretaries, and police officers at the courthouse.

When Good Grades Pay Off

While top grades may not be necessary to land your dream career, they can surely help pay the bills. A young man whom I have proudly mentored for many years, Taheed Moore, is a great example of what good grades *can* get you.

Taheed has always been a very driven young man. He knew from a young age that he wanted to go to college and become a successful financial advisor. While he was in high school, he worked diligently to get straight As because he knew he needed them to have a chance at receiving any scholarships. So, he put in the work, and he did it. Initially, he had enough scholarships to pay most of his expenses, but he did take out a loan to cover the gap for his freshman year.

His ambition never slowed, and he continued to work, head down, while attending college at Indiana University. I am proud to say he carried—and continued to carry through his entire college career—a 4.0 GPA. While I was so proud of him for working so hard and achieving those grades, I was even more proud because all of that work paid off—literally.

Taheed connected with the right people and found a group called the Norman Brown Scholars. It is an organization founded on diversity and enrichment achievement, helping students to understand diversity as a whole, as well as their origin cultures. He also found the Africana Studies Program which made him eligible to receive funding for school by adding a minor in African studies. Not only did it help pay for tuition, he was able to learn all about his culture and where he came from as a man of African descent. Both of these groups offer scholarships for those willing to dedicate some of their time and studies to culture and diversity.

With this strategic networking, paired with his straight As, Taheed was able to secure enough scholarship funds that he was actually *making* money going to school. That is pretty incredible, don't you think?

The Power of Possibility Questions:

✓ How important is my academic performance in getting accepted into college or trade school, and how much emphasis should I place on my grades in high school?

✓ How can I balance my academic performance with extracurricular activities and other experiences that can add value to my resume and make me a well-rounded candidate for potential employers?

✓ In what ways can I strategically network and connect with groups or organizations that align with my interests and goals, and how can this networking help me secure scholarships or other opportunities to support my academic and career aspirations?

CHAPTER 5

EXPERIENCE OF MENTORSHIPS

B asing your future upon a dream from childhood when you're asked "What do you want to be when you grow up" may set you up for big disappointment. The perception of what the day-to-day job looks like and the lifestyle that goes along with it can be completely disconnected from reality.

Take, for example, the perception that the lifestyle of a doctor is one of a bulky bank account and only having to work during clinic hours. This image completely overlooks the years of education necessary to even begin in the field, let alone the additional years of shadowing, working twelve-hour shifts five days a week, being on-call for medical emergencies, and the like. The payoff of success in the medical field only comes after years of dedication. Without a mentor to share these truths and experiences, this reality could come as a shock to a would-be medical student.

While it is often the goal of high school counselors and advisors to assist students in exploring a variety of career options and inspiring interests, it is often a challenge to create an encompassing experience to lead them successfully.

Mentoring is a specific strategy that should be leveraged to further explore and foster exploration in youth for their future. This is why mentorship during times of transition can be so beneficial.

Nathan is a recent college graduate who was struggling to find a job in his desired field of marketing. After months of job searching with no luck, he decided to reach out to a family friend who worked in marketing for a large corporation. This family friend, named Emily, had been in the industry for over a decade and was happy to offer guidance and support to Nathan as he navigated his job search.

Emily began meeting with Nathan regularly to discuss his job search, offer advice on his resume and cover letters, and share insights on what employers were looking for in candidates. She even introduced Nathan to a few of her colleagues in the industry who were able to offer additional guidance and connect him with job opportunities.

Thanks to Emily's guidance and mentorship, Nathan was able to secure a job at a small marketing agency. Even after he landed the job, Emily continued to be a valuable resource for him, offering advice on how to succeed in the industry and sharing her own experiences from her career.

Finding the Right Mentor

Whether it is preparing for college or trade school after high school, or beginning your first job search after high school or college, mentors can give young people a glimpse of what the educational expectations are, the competitiveness of the industry, the availability of jobs in a particular region, the ranges in pay, and the true lifestyle that comes along with it.

One study found that a positive mentoring experience was linked to career satisfaction and success for the mentee. This same study found that an ongoing pursuit of mentorship throughout an individual's career had remarkable value and increased success rates.[1]

Four types of mentors can help you transition between the Pre-Exploration Stage of your Career Life Cycle and the actual Exploration Stage once you get started. Each one brings insights for a variety of support, roles, and needs. They include:

- ➤ A Career-Specific Mentor. This type of mentor can provide advice and guidance for navigating the path toward the career of your choice. They can be a source for keeping up with current trends in the field, provide real-life answers to questions, plug you into invaluable networks, and assist in making decisions along the way.

- ➤ A Champion Mentor. This type of mentor is your personal cheerleader through every phase of your journey. They cheer you on and encourage you when you're met with obstacles or failures, and take joy along with you in your successes.

➤ A Peer Mentor. Not all mentors fit the "older and wiser" stereotype. Peer mentors create a co-mentoring relationship alongside someone who is on a similar journey to you. This relationship provides a space for supporting one another through challenges, sharing opportunities, and collaborating.

➤ An Anchor Mentor. This type of mentor provides a dependable relationship for keeping you on track during your journey. They always have your developmental goals in mind, both educational and professional, and remind you of them often. An Anchor mentor is great for reminding you of your priorities in order to stay on track and focused, especially when things get rough.[2]

So, you can see the importance of having some great mentorship in your life, but how do you go about finding a mentor?

➤ Look within your personal network: Start by considering people in your personal network who you admire and respect. This could be a family member, teacher, coach, or community leader.

➤ Use online resources: There are many online mentorship platforms and networks, such as iCouldBe and MentorCloud, which connect young people with mentors in their chosen field.

➤ Attend networking events: Attend networking events and conferences related to your interests, and make an effort to connect with people who are in positions that you aspire to.

➤ Join clubs or organizations: Join clubs or organizations related to your interests or career goals. These groups can provide opportunities to meet mentors and gain valuable insights and advice.

➤ Reach out to professional organizations: Professional organizations often have mentorship programs or can connect you with professionals in your desired field who can provide guidance and support.

Remember, when seeking a mentor, it's important to approach the relationship with an open mind and be respectful of their time and expertise. Additionally, don't be afraid to ask for help or guidance—most mentors are happy to assist young people in their journey.

The Power of Possibility Questions:

✓ How can finding a mentor benefit me in my educational and career journey?

✓ Which type of mentor could provide me with the most assistance, and why?

✓ What are some practical ways I can find a mentor in my desired field, and what steps can I take to develop a successful mentor-mentee relationship?

CHAPTER 6

VALUE OF INTERNSHIPS

I n the pursuit of your career, you'll spend countless hours in the classroom and even more studying. While these build your knowledge base and initiate peer interactions, they aren't where the most valuable skills are developed. The most valuable skills are learned during hands-on work experience with internships.

Internships provide an opportunity to interact with others and manage difficult situations in the professional environment, apply concepts learned, and work with a team to solve problems. The overall advantage of an internship experience is the opportunity to grow and prepare for your future career. Some of the other key benefits of internships include:

➤ **Networking.** It's the old adage that, "It isn't what you know, but who you know." Your newly found skills and knowledge will put you on the same level as other candidates for a career position, but knowing the right people in the right roles is what will set you apart. These relationships are where you'll learn what to expect in the real world in your career. They can also serve as role models and mentors. Not to mention, they have the ability and willingness to plug you into the right networks with the right people.

➤ **Real-Life Application.** This is your opportunity to take your new-found knowledge and skills and apply them in real-life situations. Memorizing facts, processes, and data is one thing, but the act of *doing* is what will bring everything to life.

➤ **Career Development.** Internships also afford the opportunity to grow and develop your professional etiquette, collaboration, communication skills, and so much more. It will also help you gather experience in the field for your resume.

➤ **Personal Growth.** When you begin to apply for jobs after graduation, employers will want more than just a well-educated candidate. They will be seeking out an individual that is ready to join the team and have the ability to get the job done well. Some of the key characteristics you will learn include self-motivation, integrity, and commitment.

➤ **Competitive Edge.** A survey found that college graduates who completed an internship had a starting salary of $15,000 more than those graduates who didn't. This same study found that 72.2% of college graduates with an internship experience were offered a job whereas only 36.5% of those without an internship received a job offer. Having an internship on your resume will give you a competitive advantage over other candidates.

➤ **Get Paid and Reduce Debt.** If you're fortunate, you'll find an internship that not only provides you with an invaluable experience, it will also pay. Even with a minimum wage rate, it can help you to reduce the number of expenses that add up so quickly during your pursuit of higher education.[1]

The job market is constantly changing, but one thing remains the same: employers look for candidates with work experience. In fact, one research study found that upwards of 77% of employers consider this in the recruiting process.

With that said, any internship experience will make you more attractive to potential employers. So whether the internships that are available are within your field of interest or not, paid or unpaid, the opportunity to get out there will help in your journey toward your career.

Other factors that potential employers take into consideration when comparing potential candidates are internships, volunteer activities, jobs, and leadership positions within organizations. Your experience and accomplishments in extracurricular activities can truly make you stand out from the crowd when it comes to acquiring the job of your dreams.

Landing an Internship

Finding the right internship takes time and effort. Be patient, persistent, and proactive in your search, and don't be afraid to ask for help or advice along the way.

First, check with your school. Many colleges and universities have career centers that offer information about internships. They may also have connections with companies in your field of interest.

Websites such as Indeed, Glassdoor, and LinkedIn often have internship listings. You can search for internships in your desired field, location, and even by company. Many companies have internship programs and list available positions on their websites. Check the websites of companies you are interested in and see if they offer internships.

Talk to people in your desired field and ask if they know of any internships available. Attend career fairs and industry events to meet professionals and learn about potential opportunities. Follow companies and professionals in your desired field on social media. They may post about available internship positions or share information about opportunities.

Remember, when applying for internships, it's important to tailor your application materials to the specific position and company. Be sure to highlight relevant skills and experiences and demonstrate your enthusiasm for the opportunity.

Internships of All Kinds

Earlier I introduced Shelby, a law student, and dear family friend. She had two great internship experiences that provided very different, but valuable, insights into the career world.

The first was working one-on-one with the general counsel of a hotel supply company that provides supplies like toiletries. Shelby imparted great knowledge from her mentor as she was recently fresh out of law school. Specifically, Shelby was able to glean preparation advice for her LSATs and the remainder of her journey through law school.

The second internship offered some real-world experience when the COVID pandemic hit. Shelby found herself working remotely with a technology company. She learned the value of having strong self-motivation. With the workspace evolving as it has, working remotely is something that Shelby may realistically be experiencing in her future.

I tell you about her experiences because while some internships may be directly related to your field of study, others may not be. That is not to say they aren't just as valuable and necessary to your growth as a student and a future professional.

Internships That Shape the Future

Earlier I spoke about one of my mentees, and fellow fraternity brothers, Taheed Moore. Not only did he work hard to earn some amazing financial aid, he also went on to have experiences that truly shaped his future.

During his sophomore year, he had an internship with 40|86 Advisors, which is a subsidiary of CNO Financial Group, an insurance firm. His experience allowed him to take the insurance premiums from CNO and invest them into bonds. It opened his eyes to the possibility of focusing on investments with his finance degree, something which he hadn't previously considered.

The next year he went on to work for BKD Financial Services Group which was a tax firm. There he served as a tax accountant which opened his eyes to another sector of the financial world. Later that same summer he was granted an opportunity to serve as a wealth management advisory analyst intern in Dallas, Texas. His travel and housing were all paid for, which was incredible. It gave him an experience he would have never otherwise had. It was truly a pivotal moment in his career. This internship further enhanced his interest in the investment world.

In April of 2022, I met up with Taheed at a regional conference. Knowing his interest in a future in finance and investments, I hooked him up with another one of our fraternity brothers who had connections with the executives of BMO Financial Group, which is part of a Canadian bank. These connections helped him get his foot in the door and, after some incredible networking, Taheed was offered a job coming out of college at the age of 22 with a salary of $90,000 in their corporate banking division.

At the time of this book's writing, Taheed is finishing up college and preparing to enter the working world. On the side, he is studying for his Security Industry Essentials (SIE) Exam. This will afford him the opportunity to continue pursuing his ultimate dream of working in financial investments with stocks and bonds.

Internships have the potential to open your eyes to new and different areas of focus for your career. Keeping your options open, as Taheed did, will allow you to better fully understand your future options, not to mention open doors for future success.

The Power of Possibility Questions:

✓ Which benefits of internships are most important to me and my career goals?

✓ How can I increase my chances of finding an internship that is the right fit for me? Which resources or strategies mentioned would be most useful for me?

✓ What skills and qualities can I develop through an internship, and how can I showcase those skills and qualities to potential employers in the future?

CHAPTER 7

GROWTH WITHIN GROUPS

While personal performance is paramount in your college education, this time in your life should also be viewed as an opportunity to network and improve your social and interpersonal skills. No matter if you attend a trade school, a small community college, or a large university, there are always organizations and groups to get involved with, from the Greek system, to special interest groups, to student organizations, and more.

These groups will not only expand your social skills, but they will also provide you with the chance to take on leadership and officer roles. Potential employers see these experiences as a prerequisite for highly effective employees and team members.

Involvement within a group will give you the chance to see how you and your peers handle a variety of situations. Working with a team is essential for pretty much any job you acquire after graduation. Student organizations give you the opportunity to seek advice from others, provide your own input, and collaborate with others.

You will not only get to try out your teamwork skills, you will also have the opportunity to test and expand your skills for staying organized, multi-tasking, and applying the knowledge you have acquired in your classes. Learning new skills in your coursework is extremely important, but applying those skills in the real world gives you invaluable experiences.

When looking towards the future, these groups and organizations can help to plug you into some valuable networks. Some groups will offer opportunities to interact with alumni and other professionals well into their careers which can serve you well in the future.

My daughter Tiffany was part of a historically black Greek Sorority. I encouraged her to join a sorority because of my own incredibly valuable experience with my Fraternity.

Many people think that involvement in the Greek system lasts only throughout your college years, when in fact, it continues to be a part of your life as long as you allow it. You are a member until you die. As a representative of that fraternal organization, everything you do, from the moment you joined, is living as a role model for the whole group. It is a lifelong commitment.

In this way, it is a network of individuals upon which you can call at any time and they will provide you with support. It opens up a world of possibilities, networks, and resources all around the globe. Whether you are visiting a new place and want to know the best places to visit or finding a job in a different city or industry, your Fraternity or Sorority will be there to lend a helping hand.

Tiffany found herself amongst the upper echelon of black women. They were all professionals doing amazing things, which worked as inspiration for her. Not only was she professionally inspired, the philanthropic work the sorority took part in helped her continue to grow as a woman. Their focus was on empowering other black women to get involved in helping to solve poverty, global hunger, and human trafficking. The sorority put on charity events and conferences educating their peers about the issues. This provided opportunities for Tiffany to interact with the community and network beyond the university.

Eryka took a different approach to getting involved with groups during her undergraduate years. She started her own club for black women interested in academics, called the Black Glove Society. They gathered with the goal of increasing their leadership skills and gaining experience to grow their resumes. The club participated in a variety of service jobs in area middle schools, mostly involving tutoring and mentoring students. To be even more well-rounded Eryka volunteered at area soup kitchens as well. All of this played an integral role in developing a resume her future employers couldn't ignore.

She also participated in the Minority Association for Future Attorneys as the Secretary and Recruitment Chair. For three years, even while studying abroad in England, Eryka attended and led meetings for the group. What gave her the most excitement was the exposure she received in meetings with local high schools. She enjoyed showing them that being a lawyer was an option and a goal they could reach for in their futures.

The Power of Possibility Questions:

✓ What types of groups do you hope to join in college, and what are your reasons for wanting to join those groups?

✓ How do you think these groups will contribute to your overall college experience?

✓ How will you balance your commitments to various groups with your academic and personal responsibilities in college?

✓ Have you thought about the time management skills and strategies you will need to develop in order to be an active and engaged member of your chosen groups?

CHAPTER 8

THE POWER OF ADAPTABILITY

Adaptability is a critical skill to develop during the Pre-Exploration Stage of the Career Life Cycle because it allows you to respond to new challenges and opportunities. In today's constantly changing job market, employees who are adaptable are more likely to succeed than those who are not. For example, the COVID-19 pandemic forced many companies to adopt remote working and virtual communication, and those who were able to adapt quickly were able to continue their work and maintain productivity. This is because adaptable individuals are better equipped to handle the unexpected, and are able to pivot their work in response to changing circumstances.

If you plan to pursue leadership opportunities as you enter your career, recognize that you cannot be an effective leader if you aren't adaptable. Leaders who are able to adapt to new situations and environments are better able to navigate their teams through changes and uncertainties. They are able to identify potential risks and opportunities, and adjust their strategy accordingly. This is important in today's fast-paced business environment, where companies must be able to pivot quickly to stay ahead of the competition.

Besides being important for success in the workplace, adaptability is also important for personal relationships. Those who are adaptable are better able to navigate conflicts and challenges in their relationships. They are able to see things from other people's perspectives, and are more likely to find creative solutions to problems. This is important for building strong, healthy relationships that are able to withstand the ups and downs of life.

Adaptability is also important for personal growth and development. People who are adaptable are more likely to take on new challenges and learn new skills. This is because they are not afraid of change and are willing to step outside of their comfort zone. As a result, they are more likely to grow and develop as individuals, and are more resilient in the face of adversity.

They are better able to cope with setbacks and challenges, and are less likely to experience negative emotional reactions. This is because adaptable individuals are better able to regulate their emotions and maintain a positive outlook, even in difficult situations.

Adaptability plays a role in personal fulfillment and happiness. People who are adaptable are more likely to pursue their passions and take on new challenges. They are less likely to be held back by fear or uncertainty, and are more likely to embrace new experiences and opportunities. As a result, they are more likely to lead fulfilling and satisfying lives.

Adapting to Post-High School Life

My daughter, Eryka, experienced a huge culture shock during her first year of college, and the transition was bumpy for her. Instead of focusing on school, she began adapting to the college environment in a negative way by attempting to fit in with a particular group of students. Little did she know that this group was setting themselves up on the fast track to flunking out of school. As a result of adapting her previously stellar study habits to more closely match theirs, her first semester grades were a disappointment to both herself and to us, her parents.

Eryka also found herself mixed up with a group of friends that didn't serve her focus on academics. They didn't always make the best choices, and therefore Eryka lost her way. After her first semester, she came home for break, and my wife and I knew immediately that something was wrong. Eryka wasn't acting like herself. Come to find out, when her printed grades arrived in the mail, they were the cause of her distress.

From her stellar high school grades, she had dropped to a 2.3 GPA. While Eryka is an extremely smart and adept student, her learning abilities didn't come quite as easily as they had for her sister Tiffany. Eryka thought she could breeze through college using the same skills and techniques that got her through high school. Very quickly she found it was a completely different experience that required a completely different set of skills.

Her mother and I gave her a simple, clear-cut ultimatum: she was to get back to school and work her hardest or she would be moving back home, living with us, and attending the local community college. We even drew up a contract that we all signed so our expectations were crystal clear. After many heart-to-heart conversations regarding decision-making, accountability, and consequences, Eryka pulled herself together, worked harder, and received much better grades moving forward. She ditched the unhealthy group of friends and focused her time and attention on her schooling. After that semester, she brought her GPA back up to the point where she graduated with honors.

As a college student, having clearly defined goals is essential to achieving success both in and outside of the classroom. However, it's equally important to be flexible with these goals, as college life is full of uncertainties, and it's impossible to predict every outcome. This is where the skill of adaptability comes in. The ability to adjust, course correct, and find new paths when unexpected situations or challenges arise is especially important in the college environment. It means being able to think on your feet and quickly come up with new solutions when the original plan doesn't work out.

In the college setting, being adaptable also means understanding what things can be changed and what things cannot. It's crucial to differentiate between the two as it can help you avoid unnecessary stress and anxiety. By accepting what is outside of your control, you can focus on what you can change and take action accordingly. This mindset can help you maintain a sense of calm and composure in challenging situations, allowing you to be more productive and effective in your academic pursuits.

Being adaptable in college means being willing to learn and adjust your actions and expectations as needed. As a college student, you will be faced with a variety of academic and personal challenges that may require you to adapt and find new solutions. By being open-minded and receptive to new ideas and perspectives, you can gain valuable insights and skills that can help you navigate different situations successfully.

Being adaptable also means being willing to step outside your comfort zone and take calculated risks, such as joining a new club and taking on leadership roles, as we discussed in the last chapter, or trying a new academic program. This can lead to personal growth and development, as well as open up new opportunities and possibilities that you may not have considered before.

Ultimately, adaptability is a critical skill for students to develop. The ability to adjust and find new paths when faced with unexpected situations or challenges can help you succeed academically, professionally, and personally. It allows you to maintain a sense of purpose and direction while also being flexible and open-minded. By learning how to be adaptable in college, you can become more confident with each new experience, and you will be better equipped to handle whatever challenges come your way.[1]

The most important thing to remember is that if you get on the wrong track by either failing to adapt or adapting in a way that isn't serving your best purpose, it is never too late to make the change necessary to get back on the right track. It isn't about the less-than-perfect path you took to get where you are; it's all about what you learn and how you finish.

The Power of Possibility Questions:

✓ Have you been able to adjust to unexpected situations and challenges in college?

✓ Are you willing to step outside of your comfort zone and take risks?

✓ Have you been able to maintain a sense of calm and composure in challenging situations?

CHAPTER 9

MAPPING YOUR JOURNEY

T he journey from high school to college and beyond can be overwhelming and scary at times, with moments of true uncertainty if you're headed in the right direction.

Once you've followed your educational path and received your degree or certificate for your career, it's time to begin your career search. This can be a very intimidating process. Many trade schools and community colleges offer job placement programs that can relieve this stress. Colleges and universities often offer career fairs and job search resources, so be sure to research—there is that word again—to find them and learn how to put them to good use.

My daughter, Eryka, took a unique approach to researching for her future as a lawyer. Knowing that her law school put on many networking opportunities, she made sure to attend as many as possible. It helped her to recognize the many paths that were available to her after graduating. While networking, she was able to better understand that the path to a law career wasn't always clear-cut and straight. In fact, many of her contacts helped her recognize that their paths were bumpy and full of many jobs, bouncing from one opportunity to another. This helped assuage her concerns about getting to her dream career of being an entertainment lawyer.

Eryka also went to as many job fairs as she could, even if she wasn't looking for a job. Despite her introverted nature, she learned that stepping outside of her comfort zone provided her with new contacts and information she could never find by simply researching online or in the library.

After you've dipped your toe in the water of the career search journey, you need to discover what job will be the best fit for you. Many students fresh out of college or trade school jump at the first opportunity that comes their way. While this will definitely get you out into the working world and get income flowing, it may not be in your best interest. Take a step back and recognize that you are interviewing the company for which you are applying just as much as they are interviewing you.

This is where you will need to begin researching companies. You should expect to move around and not find the perfect dream job right away. The average worker aged twenty-five to thirty-four will have four or five jobs, meaning you will move jobs about every two years. In total, the average American has about twelve jobs in their lifetime. Jobs change, as do expectations and lifestyles.[1]

It is important to research the values of an organization before considering them for a position. A third of employees that claim their values don't align with that of their organization say they are considering leaving their job.

My best piece of advice is to remember that you are never stuck on the path you start on. As we discovered throughout this booklet, so many things—opportunities, changes in life, even changes in profession choice—can steer you down a different road.

Remember to embrace the change and stay as adaptable as possible. The more open you are to the experiences that lie ahead, the more numerous your opportunities will be.

The journey toward a fulfilling and successful career can be a challenging and daunting one, but with the right mindset and strategies, it can also be an exciting and rewarding experience. By continuing to explore, learn, and grow, you can create a career path that is not only fulfilling but also meaningful and impactful.

The strategies and insights I have provided here will equip you to plan and pursue your future with open minds and hearts. Your next move is to step right into your Career Life Cycle, and I've literally written a full book about how to do that, so I invite you to pick up a copy and continue your journey!

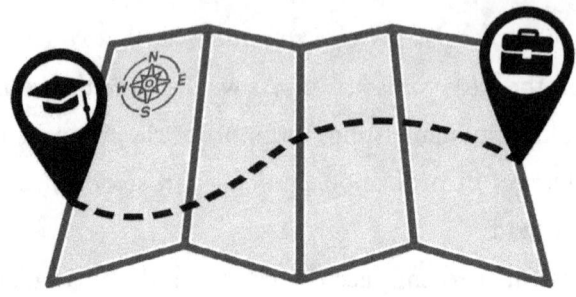

STEP 1: Pre-Exploration Stage

Find an appreciation for discipline, consistency, reliability, follow-through, and integrity.

STEP 2: Determining Life Purpose

Change your mindset to find your life purpose—a career that brings you deep joy and fulfillment.

STEP 3: Researching the Future

Research *everything*—career options within fields of interest, schools, program types, and more. Don't forget to stay open to pivoting!

STEP 4: Emphasis on Academics and Experience

Keep your head down and work hard while gathering as much experience as possible.

STEP 5: Experience of Mentorship

Find a mentor for each step of your journey and glean as much from them and their experiences as possible.

STEP 6: Value of Internship

Grow and prepare for your future career by seeking out internships of all kinds—remember experience translates over all areas of life.

STEP 7: Growth Within Groups

Get plugged into groups—expand your social and interpersonal skills while networking to show your future employers you are a highly effective employee and team member.

STEP 8: The Power of Adaptability

Set yourself up for success by living out a mindset of adaptability

ACKNOWLEDGMENTS

I want to acknowledge the following people who shared their personal experiences and inspiration during the creation of this book:

> To Charlie's Angels, my beautiful daughters, Tiffany and Eryka, for sharing your exciting journeys while pursuing careers in Medicine and Law.

> To A.J. Wilson, Shelby Wilson, Taheed Moore, and Alex Boukal for sharing your life lessons and providing different collegiate perspectives.

> I want to thank Dr. Wade A. Stevenson, Pastor—Gideon Baptist Church, for providing guidance and being a sounding board in selecting a title for this book.

ABOUT THE AUTHOR

Charles L. Jones (US Army Captain, Veteran) is principal of C&B HR Consulting and a seasoned Human Resource Executive with over 25 years of experience in Human Resources and Manufacturing Operations in Fortune 500 companies like Kraft and Mondelez International. He and his team provide human resources strategies and solutions to a wide range of businesses and nonprofits, including Intel, YWCA, and Millennium Corporation.

Learn more at cbhrconsulting.com.

END NOTES

Chapter 1

1. "US College Students Feel Unprepared for 'Real' World." VOA. https://www.voanews.com/a/us-college-students-feel-unprepared-for-real-world/3539712.html#:~:text=The%20results%20showed%2074%20percent.
2. "Bridgeport, University. "Tips for College Freshmen: Thriving as an Undecided Student." https://www.bridgeport.edu/news/tips-for-college-freshmen-and-undecided-students/#:~:text=An%20estimated%2020%2D50%25%20of.

Chapter 2

1. Coleman, John. 2022. "Finding Success Starts with Finding Your Purpose." *Harvard Business Review*, January 11, 2022. https://hbr.org/2022/01/finding-success-starts-with-finding-your-purpose.

Chapter 3

1. "2021 Community College Statistics - Data and Trends." 2021. ThinkImpact. May 10, 2021. https://www.thinkimpact.com/community-college-statistics/.
2. Warner, Andrew. 2022. Review of *5 Reasons to Consider Community College*. U.S. News. May 19, 2022. https://www.usnews.com/education/community-colleges/articles/reasons-to-consider-community-college.
3. "Average Cost of Community College by State in 2022." 2021. Research.com. December 4, 2021. https://research.com/universities-colleges/average-cost-of-community-college#:~:text=For%20the%202021%2D22%20school.
4. Bridgestock, Laura. 2018. "Top Universities." Top Universities. June 2018. https://www.topuniversities.com/student-info/student-finance/how-much-does-it-cost-study-us.

Chapter 4

1. "COVID-19: Transfer, Mobility, and Progress | National Student Clearinghouse Research Center." n.d. Nscresearchcenter.org. Accessed May 10, 2023. https://nscresearchcenter.org/transfer-mobility-and-progress/?gclid=CjwKCAjw586hBhBrEiwAQY EnHRn5Dt7XP_1XIqA9R3dz-8auvJ5LgHL6rIcIM8KGcbu_ Jm3gTV1GMRoCMm0QAvD_BwE.

Chapter 5

1. Diggs-Andrews, Kelly A., D. C. Ghislaine Mayer, and Blake Riggs. 2021. "Introduction to Effective Mentorship for Early-Career Research Scientists." *BMC Proceedings*15 (S2). https://doi.org/10.1186/s12919-021-00212-9.
2. "How College Mentors Can Foster Student Success | BestColleges." Www.bestcolleges.com. Accessed May 10, 2023. https://www.bestcolleges.com/blog/college-mentor-student-success/#:~:text=College%20mentors%20can%20offer%20professional.

Chapter 6

1. "How College Mentors Can Foster Student Success | BestColleges." Www.bestcolleges.com. Accessed May 10, 2023. https://www.bestcolleges.com/blog/college-mentor-student-success/#:~:text=College%20mentors%20can%20offer%20professional.

Chapter 8

1. Nelson, Vicki. 2014. "Going with the Flow: Why College Students' Ability to Adapt Matters." College Parent Central. October 2, 2014. https://www.collegeparentcentral.com/2014/10/going-with-the-flow-why-college-students-ability-to-adapt-matters/.

Chapter 9

1. "Average Number of Jobs in a Lifetime [2023]: How Many Jobs Does the Average Person Have – Zippia." https://www.zippia.com/advice/average-number-jobs-in-lifetime/#:~:text=On%20 average%2C%20men%20hold%2012.5.